BIOINDICATOR SPECIES

BEES
MATTER

by Erika Wassall

Content Consultant
David Inouye
Professor Emeritus, Department of Biology
University of Maryland

Core Library

An Imprint of Abdo Publishing
abdopublishing.com

abdopublishing.com

Published by Abdo Publishing, a division of ABDO, PO Box 398166, Minneapolis, Minnesota 55439. Copyright © 2016 by Abdo Consulting Group, Inc. International copyrights reserved in all countries. No part of this book may be reproduced in any form without written permission from the publisher. Core Library™ is a trademark and logo of Abdo Publishing.

Printed in the United States of America, North Mankato, Minnesota
082015
012016

THIS BOOK CONTAINS
RECYCLED MATERIALS

Cover Photo: iStockphoto
Interior Photos: iStockphoto, 1, 4, 8; Shutterstock Images, 6, 14, 16, 19, 30, 38, 40, 43, 45; Red Line Editorial/Shutterstock Images, 10; Klaus Nowottnick/Picture-Alliance/DPA/AP Images, 21; Uli Deck/DPA/Corbis, 22; Vlad Siaber/Shutterstock Images, 24; Ann Johansson/Corbis, 28; Tyler Olson/Shutterstock Images, 34; Kathy Willens/AP Images, 37

Editor: Jon Westmark
Series Designer: Laura Polzin

Library of Congress Control Number: 2015945395

Cataloging-in-Publication Data
Wassall, Erika.
 Bees matter / Erika Wassall.
   p. cm. -- (Bioindicator species)
ISBN 978-1-68078-008-6 (lib. bdg.)
Includes bibliographical references and index.
1. Bees--Juvenile literature. 2. Bee ecology--Juvenile literature.   3. Environmental protection--Juvenile literature.   I. Title.
595.79--dc23

                                                      2015945395

CONTENTS

CHAPTER ONE

BEES AS BIOINDICATORS

A swarm of honeybees hovers over a hillside of flowering plants. Blossoms extend out long, skinny structures, called stamens. Tiny powder-like grains, called pollen, cling to the ends of the stamens. The bees gather food from the flowers for their hive. At each blossom, pollen sticks to the bees' hairy bodies. The insects dart from flower to flower. Pollen spreads among the plants.

Stamens stick out from flowers to help spread pollen.

Some bees, such as honeybees and bumblebees, carry pollen with the flat parts of their hind legs, called pollen baskets.

The Great Relationship

Many plants need pollen from other plants of the same species to reproduce. They rely on pollinators, such as bees, to help with this. Pollination allows plants to produce fruits and vegetables. These contain seeds that may become new plants. Nectar attracts bees to flowers. Nectar is a sugary liquid made by plants. Bees use nectar and pollen for food and to make honey. As bees take nectar from flowering plants, they spread pollen.

Bees and plants are interdependent. This means that both living things need each other to survive. Without bees many plants would die. And bees would starve without plants. The relationship is part of the balance of the natural world.

Busy Bees

Honeybees can travel up to six miles (10 km) from the hive. On each trip, a bee can gather pollen from 75 to 100 flowers. One bee can make 12 to 15 flights per day. Bees always return to the same hive. Inside every hive is a queen bee. The queen keeps the hive healthy by laying eggs. A single queen bee can lay up to 2,000 eggs in one day.

The number of bees in a hive changes throughout the year. In summer a hive can house more than 80,000 bees. With such high numbers of bees, a hive can collect pollen from more than 500 million flowers in a year. Bees use the pollen to feed growing bees.

Beekeepers keep bees in man-made hives. Cold winters can greatly reduce hive populations.

8

They use nectar to make honey. The bees store up the honey to eat during winter.

Winter is a hard season for bees. The number of bees in an average hive drops to approximately 25,000. Bees spend winter keeping themselves and the queen alive. The queen slows or stops laying eggs. The bees group together, fluttering their wings and moving around. Clusters help bees stay warm. Bees take turns being on the outside of the cluster. But the queen always stays at the center, where it is warmest. Bees do not leave the hive in winter.

PERSPECTIVES
Beekeepers

Beekeepers rely on bees for their livelihood. Winter is hard on bees. And bees dying from cold winters is part of beekeeping. As much as an 18 percent loss is often thought of as acceptable. But when beekeepers lose 40 or 50 percent of their hives in a single season, it is a big blow to their income. Keeping bees and hives healthy can be expensive.

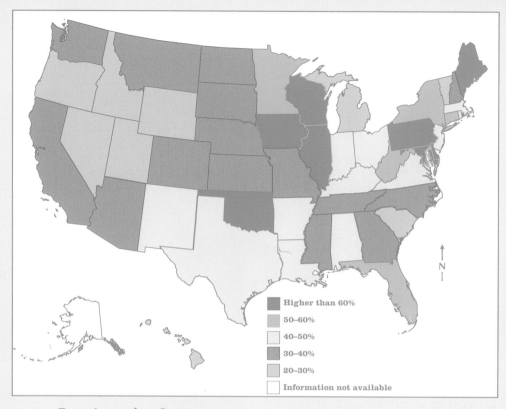

Bee Loss by State

This map of the United States shows the percentage of hives that died in each state from 2014 to 2015. How does hive loss vary around the country? What areas have the highest hive loss?

It is not uncommon in very cold winters for some colonies to die off. But other factors can make hives more vulnerable.

Bees interact with many plants in their environment. Bees are also sensitive to small changes. These two things make them excellent bioindicators.

A bioindicator is a species that gives humans information about the health of its ecosystem. The health of a bee colony helps people understand the health of the world around it.

Bees on the Decline

Since the early 1900s, the populations of many types of bees have been dropping. A number of species are endangered. Some are even believed to be extinct. One endangered species is the Franklin's bumblebee. This type of bee was once common in Northern California. Warming temperatures and loss of habitat started to hurt the bumblebee's ecosystem in the mid-1990s. Between 1998 and 2001, sightings of Franklin's bumblebees dropped greatly. The bees are now near extinction throughout the Pacific Northwest.

Between the 1940s and 2015, the number of honeybee colonies in the United States dropped from 5 million to 2.5 million. In the winter of 2006, more than 30 percent of US honeybee colonies were lost.

The loss was two times the expected drop. Winter losses have remained higher than normal since.

As bee populations drop, many plants also die. Orchid flowers in the Amazon rain forest are one example. Many orchids in this region need a specific type of bee for pollination. If those bees die, the orchids are not able to reproduce.

Bee health indicates the health of the surrounding environment. And when an ecosystem breaks down, all living things are affected, including humans.

Colony Collapse Disorder

A set of symptoms leading to empty hives has been named Colony Collapse Disorder (CCD). The causes of CCD are unclear. Colonies that might have recently seemed healthy can be affected. Beekeepers find the hives mysteriously empty, undamaged, and often with no signs of illness. Worker bees are gone. These are the bees that gather food. When worker bees stop coming back to the hive, the colony collapses. Any bees left behind do not survive.

Bees help us make a variety of products. The following passage is from an article by the US Food and Drug Administration about the important products bees create:

> Honey, of course, is the most well-known and economically important hive product. . . . After honey, beeswax is the second most important hive product from an economic standpoint. . . . Beeswax is popular for making candles and as an ingredient in artists' materials and in leather and wood polishes. . . . Beeswax is also one of the most commonly used waxes in cosmetics. . . .
>
> But the greatest importance of honey bees to agriculture isn't a product of the hive at all. It's their work as crop pollinators. This agricultural benefit of honey bees is estimated to be between 10 and 20 times the total value of honey and beeswax. Honey bees are like flying dollar bills buzzing over U.S. crops.
>
> Source: "Helping Agriculture's Helpful Honey Bees: Drugs to Control American Foulbrood." FDA.gov. US Food and Drug Administration, January 2015. Web. Accessed April 15, 2015.

What's the Big Idea?

Read the passage carefully. What is the main idea? How is that main idea supported by details? Name two or three of these supporting details.

CHAPTER TWO

A DIFFERENT WORLD

Within only a few decades, much has changed for bees. In the 1940s, farmers made up approximately 20 percent of the US workforce. By 1990 the number of farmers had dropped to 2.6 percent. Over the same period, the total number of farms dropped from 6 million to 2.5 million. Meanwhile, the number of people in the United States went up. The population is now more

The growing human population has increased the need for crops, such as corn.

Farmers grow soybeans to feed animals and produce food products, such as vegetable oil.

than 318 million, compared to 132 million in the 1940s. With many more people to feed, the average farm size has nearly tripled.

A Changing World

The farming change that took place in the 1940s was called the Green Revolution. During this time, monocrop farms became more common. Instead of growing many types of crops, farmers began to grow only one crop on their farms. This allowed farmers to specialize in one type of crop. Monocrop farms had higher yields. This helped feed the growing population.

Today monocrop farms are even more common. Approximately half of the farm fields in the United States grow only corn or soybeans. Farmers also use more chemicals to protect their crops from weeds, diseases, and pests.

Crop yields are high as a result. And the streamlined process allows foods to be sold at a lower cost. However, these practices have also changed the farm landscape.

Corn in Our Cars

In 2013 US farmers planted 97.4 million acres (39 million ha) of corn. Much of that corn was never eaten. Forty percent of US cornfields are used to make ethanol. Ethanol is added to gasoline to help it burn cleaner. Farmers grow huge fields of corn to meet demand. Bees cannot survive feeding only on corn plants. As different types of fuels are developed, the need for ethanol may go down. This could allow farmers to plant more types of crops.

A Bee's Perspective

Honeybees need variety in their diets. They prefer to get most of their food within 2.5 miles (4 km) of the hive. In the past, finding the needed nutrition was easy. Farms had plenty of wild growth and types of crops. With monocrop farming, hundreds of acres may grow a single crop. Bees struggle to get the nutrients they need. There

Pesticides can keep harmful insects off of plants, but the chemicals can also harm other living things.

are not other food sources nearby when the single crop is done flowering.

Pesticides are also a problem for bees. Farmers use pesticides to protect their crops from harmful insects. But the chemicals can also kill bees. Levels of toxins that do not kill bees can still destroy colonies. The chemicals can change the ways bees act. In 2014 scientists studied a pesticide's effect on bumblebees. The chemical did not kill bees right away. Instead their growth slowed. Many could no longer find their way back to the hive. Without enough food, entire hives broke down.

Natural Illness

A type of parasite adds to bees' challenges. The *Varroa destructor* mite quickly spread across the United States in the 1980s. The mite is no bigger than the tip of a pin. But it has become a huge problem for beekeepers. Varroa mites bite bees, suck their blood, and spread disease.

Varroa mites were likely shipped to the United States with honeybees from Brazil. The mites are an invasive species. Invasive species are organisms that are not naturally found in an area and that hurt the native organisms.

Illnesses are not new in the bee world. There are many other parasites and diseases that can affect a colony. Dysentery, chalkbrood, bacterial diseases, and starvation can destroy hives. But American honeybees did not evolve with the threat of varroa mites. The

Varroa mites weaken bees and shorten their life spans.

bees do not have protection against these dangerous parasites. Many US hives died before beekeepers understood the problem. Beekeepers must now regularly inspect their hives. The keepers must plan in advance how to fight the destructive mite.

Beekeepers must monitor their hives to make sure varroa mites do not spread throughout colonies.

Treatments are available for varroa mites. But fighting off illness can leave hives vulnerable to other stressors.

The Deadly Combination

There are still mysteries surrounding what contributes most to hive failure. However, the picture is becoming clearer. Many human-created factors affect bee health.

A deadly combination of human practices is at the heart of the bee decline. These factors combine to put extra stress on bees. Better understanding the ways in which humans affect bees not only helps bees but entire ecosystems.

EXPLORE ONLINE

The Green Revolution was originally a new farming method to help poor farmers grow more crops. But the movement led to the use of more pesticides and single-crop farms. The website link below covers the pros and cons of the Green Revolution. How is the information on the website similar to the information in Chapter Two? What new information did you learn from the website?

The Green Revolution
mycorelibrary.com/bees-matter

CHAPTER THREE

LIVING WITHOUT BEES?

As pollinators, bees have important jobs. Flowering plants count on them for reproduction and for growing fruits and vegetables. Fruits and vegetables are an important food source for larger animals. In this way, threats to bee health affect all living things in an ecosystem. Since bees are bioindicators, their decline warns of a larger problem.

Multiple bees must visit a single cucumber plant in order for it to successfully grow vegetables.

Crop	US Value (Billions)	Percent Pollinated by Honeybees
Soybeans	$40.3	50
Alfalfa	$10.8	60
Almonds	$6.5	100
Cotton	$5.1	80
Apples	$3.0	90
Oranges	$2.0	90
Sweet cherries	$0.8	90
Peaches	$0.6	80
Tangerines	$0.5	90
Grapefruits	$0.2	90

More than Honey

This chart shows to what degree US crops depend on honeybees. It also shows how much each crop was worth in 2014. How does this chart help you understand the importance of bees for food production?

Variety Lost

Today going through the produce section of a grocery store is a colorful experience. The aisles are full of different smells and textures. But the experience would be much more dreary without bees to pollinate plants. Many beautiful and delicious foods would be scarce.

Without bees refrigerators would be without apples. Kitchens would not be stocked with coffee beans. Even dairy products would be affected. Dairy cows eat alfalfa and clover. These plants count on leaf-cutter bees, bumblebees, and honeybees for pollination.

Alternatives to Natural Pollination

With fewer bees, some farmers try other ways of pollinating. Some practice pollen dusting. In this method, farmers spray pollen over a field from an aircraft. Pollen dusting is not often used because of its high cost. It also produces a lower percentage of fruit.

Other farmers pollinate by hand because there are not enough bees. Some apple farmers in China pollinate their crops using tiny paintbrushes. This method leads to a huge increase in the cost of apples. People cannot afford such large increases in food costs. Also, there are not enough people to hand-pollinate all crops.

Beekeepers bring hives to California from across the country in order to pollinate huge almond orchards.

Migratory Beekeeping

A growing number of farmers are using migratory beekeepers. Migratory beekeeping is when hives are loaded onto trucks and sent to farms. Farmers pay per hive. They schedule to have the bees shipped in for pollination season.

Migratory beekeeping allows a single bee to pollinate in many areas. Almond blossoms in California require huge numbers of bees. Beekeepers bring honeybees from all over the country for the job.

Those same bees are shipped to Michigan to pollinate blueberries in the summer. In the fall, they may travel to Texas to pollinate pumpkins.

This can have harmful effects on the bees. Like all animals, there are natural patterns in a bee's life. Living in different parts of the country in a single year can change these patterns. Shipping bees can also spread illnesses that could have been kept in one area. Even with careful transport, hives can become stressed and weak.

PERSPECTIVES
World's Largest Bee Migration

Every year more than half of all honeybees across the United States are shipped to California to pollinate almonds. The state has more than 1,000 square miles (2,590 sq km) of almond trees. And almond flowers have only a five-day window for pollination. It takes a huge number of bees to do the job. Farmers pay up to $200 for each hive. With more than 1.5 million hives needed, the cost quickly adds up. This high price gets passed on to people who buy almonds at the store.

Fewer bees could bring about higher prices at the grocery store.

Money Matters

Pollination once happened without farmers giving it a second thought. But without healthy local bees, many farmers must find other ways to grow their crops.

This adds a new side to farm management. Farmers may keep their own bees, bring in hives, or even change crops. Any action takes time and money.

Around the world, people demand affordable food. Farmers compete to grow crops that can be sold at lower prices. But as bee populations drop, the cost of nuts, fruits, and vegetables will continue to rise.

The Realistic Outlook

It is unlikely that bees will die off completely. But there are big concerns on the horizon. If bee numbers keep dropping, many plants will become hard to find and too costly to grow. Eating a healthy diet may become more difficult for families around the world.

The Global Threat of Habitat Loss

Bees are far from the only animal suffering from habitat loss. Habitat loss is when the natural ecosystem of an animal is changed and no longer supports that animal's needs. When one animal is affected, animals that depend on it are also affected. Habitat loss is considered by many to be the world's biggest threat to wildlife.

Beyond the Bees

The falling bee population indicates environmental changes that could have widespread effects. When bees are exposed to chemicals such as pesticides, other creatures are also likely exposed. Predators, such as hawks, feed on small animals. Hawks can become sick if they eat animals containing high levels of pesticides. Rain can wash pesticides into ponds and rivers. The chemicals can kill off frogs, fish, and water insects. Animals that count on these animals for food also suffer.

Shrinking bee numbers can be the first sign the health of an ecosystem is in danger. Studying bees is one way scientists can recognize areas that are at risk.

This excerpt is from "The Buzz on Native Bees," an article published during National Pollinator Week in 2013 by the US Geological Survey:

> Native bees pollinate native plants like cherries, blueberries and cranberries, and were here long before European honey bees were brought to the country by settlers. Honey bees, of course, are well known for pollinating almond and lemon trees, okra, papaya and watermelon plants. But native bees are estimated to pollinate 80 percent of flowering plants around the world. And very few of them sting—really!
>
> According to the [US Department of Agriculture], bees of all sorts pollinate approximately 75 percent of the fruits, nuts and vegetables grown in the United States, and one out of every four bites of food people take is courtesy of bee pollination. In sum, bee pollination is responsible for more than $15 billion in increased crop value each year.
>
> Source: Hannah Hamilton. "The Buzz on Native Bees." USGS.gov. US Department of the Interior, November 2013. Web. Accessed April 15, 2015.

Back It Up

This author uses evidence to support a point. Write a paragraph describing the point the author is making. Then list two or three pieces of evidence the author uses to support her point.

CHAPTER FOUR

PLANNING A BRIGHTER FUTURE

The bee population around the globe is dropping. The good news is humans can do much to change the trend. Big changes are already being made to help bees. Bee numbers are still going down but have started to level out around the world.

Beekeeping Practices

Honeybees' first line of defense is the people caring for them—the beekeepers. The challenges facing

Beekeepers can carefully monitor bees to understand how a population is doing.

Rooftop Hives

Beekeepers do not need to live in rural areas. Hives take up only a few square feet. Urban beekeeping has become common. In Atlanta, Chicago, Denver, San Francisco, Seattle, and many more cities, beekeepers have set up rooftop hives with honeybees. In 2010 New York City lifted a ban on beekeeping. And in 2015, Los Angeles received growing support for allowing backyard beekeeping.

honeybees have changed. Beekeepers' management practices must also change. Regular checks for parasites and illness are important. Quick and proper treatment can save colonies.

Hive health is now tracked across the United States through the Bee Informed Partnership. Beekeepers voluntarily report on their colonies throughout the year. Keeping an eye on bee numbers and health helps guide protective actions.

Government Intervention

Since 2007, National Pollinator Week has highlighted the importance of bees. Tours, honey tastings, educational hikes, and other family-friendly activities

People have started beekeeping in big cities to promote bee health.

allow for a firsthand understanding of pollinators. The US government created The Pollinator Health Task Force in 2014. In May 2015, the task force released a national strategy to promote the health of bees and other pollinators. The strategy lays out plans for bee research, public outreach, and land management.

Proper Use of Chemicals

People can lower the harmful effects of pesticides by using them at the proper time and using the correct

Without harmful pesticides, bees are better able to pollinate crops.

method. These things are based on the natural cycles of surrounding plants and animals.

The labels of some pesticides are being rewritten to help protect bees. For example, some labels will tell farmers to apply pesticides only after the plants have flowered and the petals have fallen. This gives bees time to gather nectar and pollen before any chemicals are applied.

Sustainable Farming

Sustainable farming is a way to grow food through techniques that help the environment. These methods are becoming more common. Nationwide programs are researching the side effects of monocrop farming. The goal is to understand its effects and develop alternatives to pesticides.

Biopesticides are one alternative. These are chemicals made with only natural ingredients. Biopesticides pose less of a threat to pollinators and are gaining popularity.

Small Changes Add Up

Everyone can make decisions that help bees. Homeowners can plant flowers that attract pollinators. People can avoid spraying unnecessary chemicals

Planting flower gardens attracts bees and other important pollinators, such as butterflies.

around their properties. Doing these things helps bees that visit gardens and yards. People can buy produce from organic farms. These types of farms grow food with natural pest-control methods and promote plant diversity.

The Future

Low bee populations show that the ecosystem has been disrupted. This message is finally being heard. If people continue to take steps to protect bees, bee numbers can be stabilized. The relationship between bees, plants, and the ecosystem as a whole can be restored. As the bee population gains strength, the plants flourish. In turn the plants provide nutrients to humans and other animals that rely on them.

Bees matter. Bees keep food in our farm fields, our grocery stores, and our stomachs. Healthy bees not only feed the world. They also foretell the future of many living things within an ecosystem.

FURTHER EVIDENCE

Chapter Four discusses what is being done to protect bees. What were the main points of this chapter? What evidence can you find supporting these points? Read the article from the website below. Find two pieces of information to support the main ideas of Chapter Four.

Good News for Bees
mycorelibrary.com/bees-matter

Common Names: Bees, bumblebees, honeybees, carpenter bees, leaf-cutter bees

Scientific Name: Apoidea

Color: Range from brown and yellow to green and blue

Average Life Span: Honeybees live 6 months to 1 year, with queens living 3 to 5 years. Bumblebees live 3 to 6 weeks, with queens living 1 year.

Diet: Pollen and nectar from flowers

Habitat: Areas with a variety of flowering vegetation

Predators: Birds, small mammals, reptiles, and insects

What's Happening: The honeybee population has been cut in half since the 1940s, and we also have fewer bumblebees and orchid bees, among others.

Where It's Happening: Bee numbers are dropping all around the world.

Why It's Happening: Stressors such as pesticides, diseases, and lack of nutrition are making bees vulnerable.

Why It's Important: Bees pollinate a variety of the plants that produce food for humans and animals. Struggling

bees also indicate that broad problems, such as habitat loss and pesticide misuse, are becoming common issues for animals around the world.

What You Can Do:

- Encourage minimal chemical use around your yard. Use organic alternatives when possible.
- Plant a bee garden with flowering plants to attract bees.
- Buy local honey. This helps support someone who is looking out for bee health.

Take a Stand

Monocrop farming allows for large amounts of food to be grown at a cheaper cost, helping to feed the world. But it can also have negative effects on ecosystems. What are the pros and cons of this type of farming? Do you think growing food this way is a good idea? Why or why not?

Why Do I Care?

Bees pollinate food that we all eat. How would your daily diet be affected if there were no bees? What are some of your favorite fruits and vegetables? How would your life be different if you could no longer find or afford the foods you like to eat?

Dig Deeper

After reading this book, what questions do you
still have about bees? With an adult's help, find a
few reliable sources that can help you answer your
questions. Write a paragraph about what you learned.

You Are There

This book discusses the decline of bees around the
world. Imagine you are a farmer. Write a letter to your
friends about your concerns for the bee population
and what it will mean for your crops this year. What
decisions will you have to make, and what will it mean
for your final crops?

GLOSSARY

interdependent
a relationship where two living things rely on each other to survive

migratory
consistently moving from one place to another

monocrop
growing only one type of crop

nectar
a sugary liquid produced by flowers

parasite
an organism that lives and feeds on another organism, causing it harm

pesticides
a substance used to kill pests

pollen
tiny powder-like grains that help flowers reproduce

pollination
the transfer of pollen from one plant to another

yield
the amount of crops produced from a unit of land

LEARN MORE

Books

Huber, Raymond. *Flight of the Honey Bee.*
    Somerville, MA: Candlewick Press, 2013.

Rotner, Shelley, and Anne Woodhull. *The Buzz on*
    Bees: Why Are They Disappearing? New York:
    Holiday House, 2010.

Winchester, Elizabeth. *Time for Kids: Bees!* New
    York: HarperCollins, 2005.

Websites

To learn more about Bioindicator Species, visit
booklinks.abdopublishing.com. These links are
routinely monitored and updated to provide the most
current information available.

Visit **mycorelibrary.com** for free additional tools for
teachers and students.

INDEX

ABOUT THE AUTHOR

Erika Wassall is an author, entrepreneur, and farmer. She is a member of the New Jersey Beekeepers Association and a lover of bees. Wassall lives with her husband on a small farm. They raise vegetables, sheep, chickens, and pigs.